+<=[A Math]~±÷

A Math Journey Through the HUMAN BODY

Anne Rooney

Crabtree Publishing Company
www.crabtreebooks.com

Crabtree Publishing Company
www.crabtreebooks.com
1-800-387-7650

Published in Canada
616 Welland Ave.
St. Catharines, ON
L2M 5V6

Published in the United States
PMB 59051, 350 Fifth Ave.
59th Floor,
New York, NY

Published in 2015 by CRABTREE PUBLISHING COMPANY.

First published in 2014 by Wayland
(A division of Hachette Children's Books)

Author: Anne Rooney
Commissioning editor: Debbie Foy
Editorial director: Kathy Middleton
Content Review: Reagan Miller
Editors: Jon Richards, Crystal Sikkens
Consultant: Steve Winney
Designer: Ed Simkins
Prepress technician: Katherine Berti
Print and production coordinator: Katherine Berti

Produced by Tall Tree Ltd

Photographs:
4-5 Shutterstock.com / Gelpi JM, 5cl Shutterstock.com / James Steidl, 6tl Shutterstock.com / fotofreaks, 9br Shutterstock.com / Eduard Stelmakh, 10-11 all Shutterstock.com / Valery121283, 13t Shutterstock.com / Lukiyanova Natalia / frenta, 14tr, 17bc Shutterstock.com / Lucy Liu, 14c and 15 cr Shutterstock / com / siamionau pavel, 14bl Shutterstock.com / Image Point Fr, 14br, 15tr Shutterstock.com / Preto Perola, 15c Shutterstock.com / Shutter_M, 16tr, 17tr Shutterstock.com / PRILL, 16-17 Shutterstock.com / chaoss, 19tr Shutterstock.com / jannoon028, 19br Shutterstock.com / udaix, 22tr, 29tr Shutterstock.com / Veronica Louro, 27c Shutterstock.com / Jason Winter, cover Shutterstock.com

Printed in Hong Kong / 082014 / BK20140613

Library and Archives Canada Cataloguing in Publication

Rooney, Anne, author
A math journey through the human body / Anne Rooney.

(Go figure!)
Includes index.
Issued in print and electronic formats.
ISBN 978-0-7787-0734-9 (bound).--ISBN 978-0-7787-1459-0 (pbk.).--
ISBN 978-1-4271-7667-7 (pdf).--ISBN 978-1-4271-7663-9 (html)

1. Mathematics--Juvenile literature. 2. Human body--Juvenile literature. I. Title.

QA40.5.R665 2014 j510 C2014-903582-9
C2014-903583-7

Library of Congress Cataloging-in-Publication Data

Rooney, Anne, author.
A math journey through the human body / Anne Rooney.
pages cm. -- (Go figure!)
Includes index.
ISBN 978-0-7787-0734-9 (reinforced library binding) -- ISBN 978-0-7787-1459-0 (pbk.) -- ISBN 978-1-4271-7667-7 (electronic pdf) -- ISBN 978-1-4271-7663-9 (electronic html)
1. Mathematics--Juvenile literature. 2. Human body--Juvenile literature. 3. Human body--Miscellanea--Juvenile literature. I. Title.

QA113.R656 2015
510--dc23

2014020137

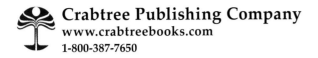

go figure!

With the help of an amazing robot, you are about to go on a mathematical tour of the human body.

CONTENTS

04 YOUR WHOLE BODY

06 EATING WELL

08 BREATHE IN, BREATHE OUT

10 HEAVY LIFTING

12 MEASURE ME

14 COMPARING BODIES

16 SKIN SURFACES

18 BARE BONES

20 BODY RATIOS

22 BIGGER AND BIGGER

24 TRIANGLES INSIDE YOU!

26 SHARING DATA

28 ANSWERS

30 MATH GLOSSARY

32 LEARNING MORE AND INDEX

Words in **bold** appear in the glossary on pages 30–31.

Answers to the Go Figure! challenges can be found on page 28.

Please note: The Imperial and the metric systems are used interchangeably throughout this book.

WHAT EQUIPMENT DO YOU NEED?

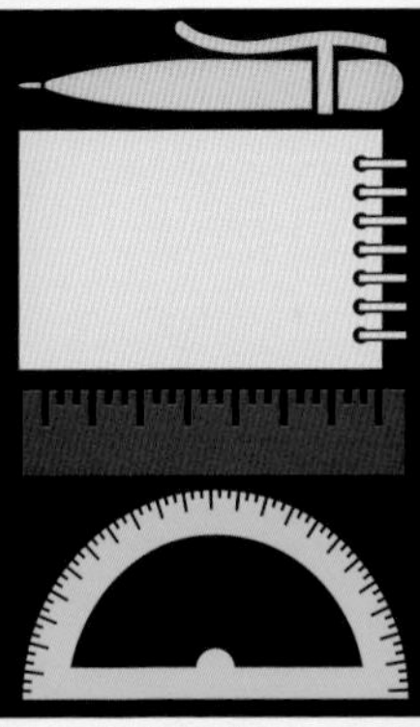

Pen or pencil

Notepad

Ruler

Protractor

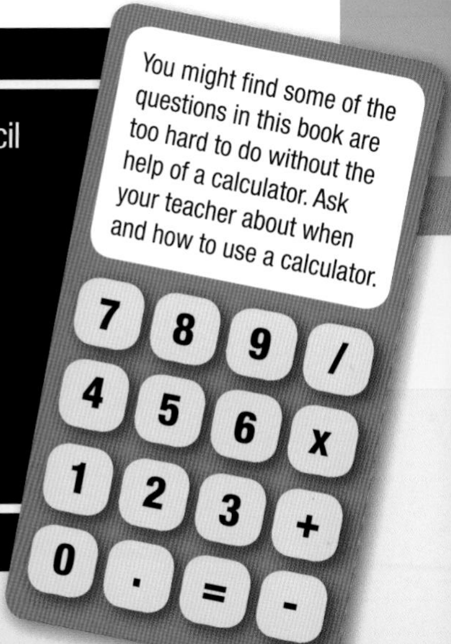
You might find some of the questions in this book are too hard to do without the help of a calculator. Ask your teacher about when and how to use a calculator.
7 8 9 /
4 5 6 x
1 2 3 +
0 . = -

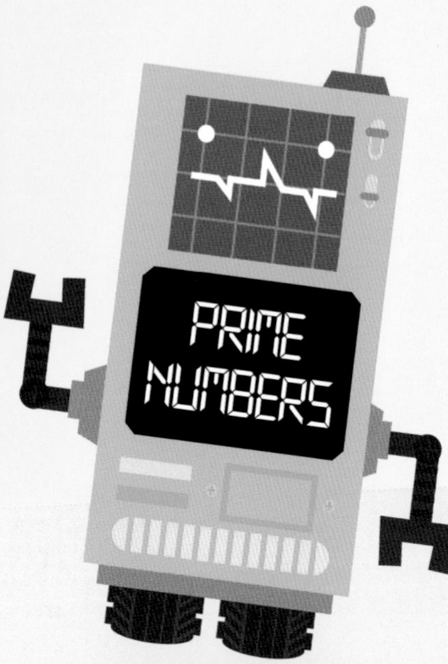

YOUR WHOLE BODY

You are doing a study of the human body. A robot called Andrew is helping you to take measurements and collect data.

Numbers are related to each other in various ways, such as whether they are odd or even, or if they have factors**.**

LEARN ABOUT IT
NUMBER SENSE

All numbers except zero are either odd or even. **Even numbers** can be divided by 2 and give an answer that is a whole number. If you **add** two even or two **odd numbers** together, the answer is always even. If you add an odd and an even number together, the answer is always odd.

The factor of a number is a whole number that can be divided exactly into it. You can divide 12 exactly by 3 (to get 4), so 3 is a factor of 12.

The factors of 12 are 1, 2, 3, 4, 6, and 12:

$12 \div 1 = 12$

$12 \div 2 = 6$

$12 \div 4 = 3$

A number that has no factors except itself and 1 is called a **prime number**. The first ten prime numbers are:

2, 3, 5, 7, 11, 13, 17, 19, 23, 29

All numbers can be split up by **place values** into ones, tens, hundreds, and so on:

Thousands	Hundreds	Tens	Ones	
2	6	3	7	2000+ 600+ 30+ 7 2,637
9	0	3	4	9,000+ 30+ 4 9,034

›GO FIGURE!

Andrew likes numbers. He has listed some numbers having to do with your body, and challenged you to a numbers quiz:

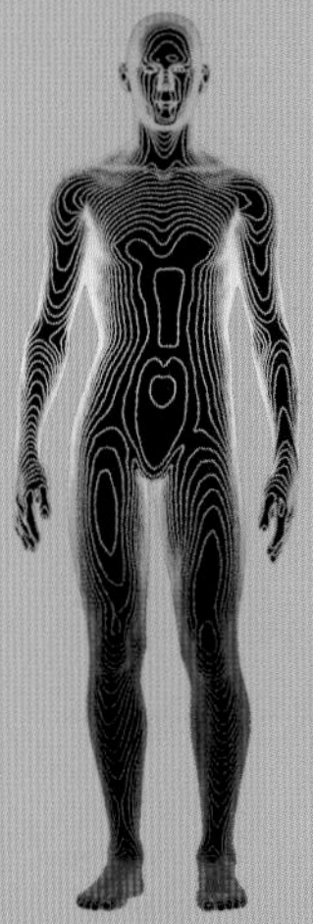

Fingers (each hand)	5
Teeth	26
Eyes	2
Nose	1
Limbs	4
Lungs	2
Hairs	285,324
Eyelashes	467

1. Which of these figures are prime numbers?
2. What are the factors of 26?
3. If you added the number of eyelashes to the number of hairs, would the answer be odd or even?
4. What is the figure in the ten thousands place in the number of hairs and what is its value?
5. How would you write the number of hairs in a place value chart using ones, tens, hundreds, and so on?

MISSION 2

EATING WELL

You want to check if you are eating enough healthy foods, so Andrew has kept track of the fruit and vegetables you have eaten during one week.

LEARN ABOUT IT
WORK WITH TABLES AND BAR GRAPHS

Data **is sometimes shown in** tables **or** bar graphs**. Often, you will start with data you have collected and make a table and then a bar graph.**

To make a bar graph from a table, you need to choose one part of the data to plot along the x **axis** (the bottom of the graph) and another for the y axis (going up the graph). The data for the y axis must be numbers to show the amount.

This table shows the number of children in a class who have visited the dentist in a three-month period.

Month	Dentist visits
April	13
May	7
June	10

This bar graph shows the same data:

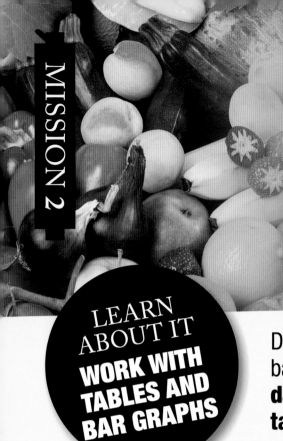

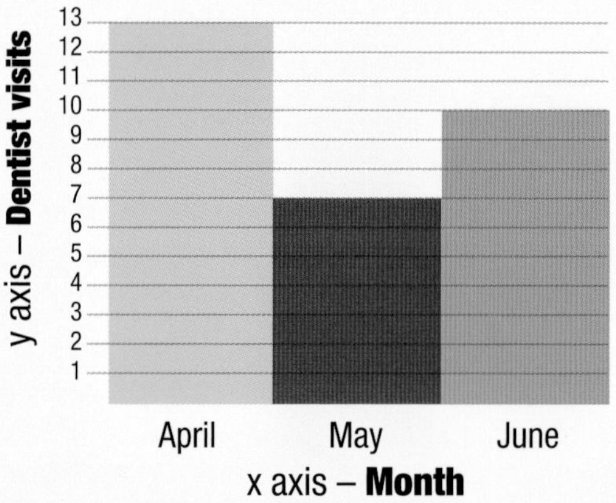

There is a bar for each month. The height of the bar shows the number of children who visited the dentist that month.

›GO FIGURE!

This is a table showing the vegetable servings you have eaten:

Day	Vegetable servings
Monday	3
Tuesday	2
Wednesday	2
Thursday	1
Friday	2
Saturday	3
Sunday	2

This is a bar graph showing the fruit servings you have eaten:

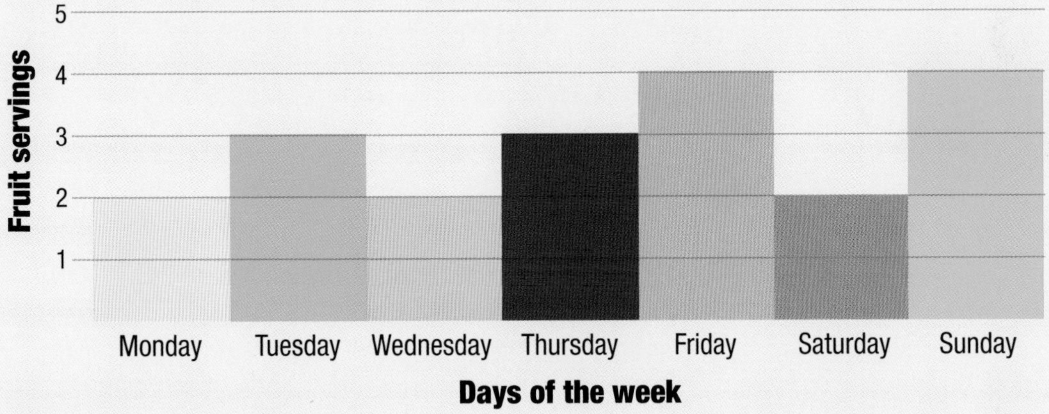

1. On which days did you only have three fruit servings?
2. Which days did you have fewest fruit servings?
3. In your notepad, draw a bar graph to show how many vegetable servings you ate during the week.
4. On which days did you have more vegetables than fruit?
5. Which of the tables below show the same data as the bar graph for fruit?

A

Day	Fruit servings
Monday	2
Tuesday	3
Wednesday	2
Thursday	3
Friday	4
Saturday	2
Sunday	4

B

Day	Fruit servings
Monday	2
Tuesday	3
Wednesday	2
Thursday	4
Friday	3
Saturday	2
Sunday	4

BREATHE IN, BREATHE OUT

You want to compare the gases you breathe out with the gases you breathe in. To do this, you are blowing up balloons and Andrew is measuring the different gases inside them.

LEARN ABOUT IT PERCENTAGES

You can think of percentages **as being the same as hundredths. The whole of something is 100 percent (%), or $^{100}/_{100}$. Half of something is 50 percent, or $^{50}/_{100}$. Percentages must always add up to 100.**

An adult's lungs can hold about 5 liters of air. However, when an adult breathes normally, he or she will only breathe in about 0.5 liters of air. To find out what percentage of the total volume this is, divide the air breathed in by the volume of the lungs and multiply by 100:

$$\frac{0.5}{5} = 0.1 \times 100 = 10\%$$

When an adult takes in a deep breath, he or she will breathe in about 60 percent of their total lung volume. You can work out the volume of this deep breath using the following **equation**:

$$\frac{60}{100} \times 5 = \text{volume of breath}$$

$$0.6 \times 5 = 3 \text{ liters}$$

›GO FIGURE!

Andrew has printed this table showing the percentages of different gases in the air that you breathe in and out. But he has not been able to record some of the figures and has marked them with an "X."

BREATHING IN	
Nitrogen	**78%**
Oxygen	**X%**
Other gases	**1%**

BREATHING OUT	
Nitrogen	**78%**
Oxygen	**16%**
Carbon dioxide	**X%**
Other gases	**1%**

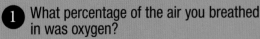

1. What percentage of the air you breathed in was oxygen?

2. What percentage of the gases you breathed out was carbon dioxide?

3. In your notepad, draw a bar graph to show the proportion of gases in the air you breathed out.

4. The total volume of air you breathed in was 600 cm^3 of air. How many cm^3 of oxygen did you breathe in?

MISSION 4

HEAVY LIFTING

Andrew has been helping you to work out how strong you are compared to your friends. You are putting bags of fruit and vegetables into a box, and he is recording how much you can lift and carry a short distance.

LEARN ABOUT IT
MIXED OPERATIONS

Often, a problem involves more than one operation (adding, subtracting**, multiplying, or dividing). You need to do them in the right order.**

If you buy two drinks that cost 75 cents each and three apples that cost 30 cents each, the total cost is:

(2 X $0.75) + (3 X $0.30) = $1.50 + $0.90 = $2.40

Do the parts of the problem inside the brackets first. If you wrote the problem without brackets it would look like this:

2 X $0.75 + 3 X $0.30

If you see a problem like this, do the multiplication and division first and then do any addition and subtraction. If you did the addition first in this problem, you would not get the correct answer.

2 X $3.75 X $0.30 = $2.25

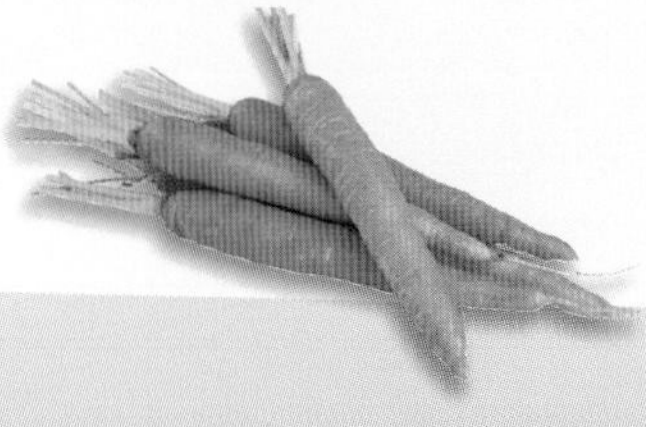

›GO FIGURE!

The food comes in paper bags and you are going to carry them in a box that weighs 200 g.

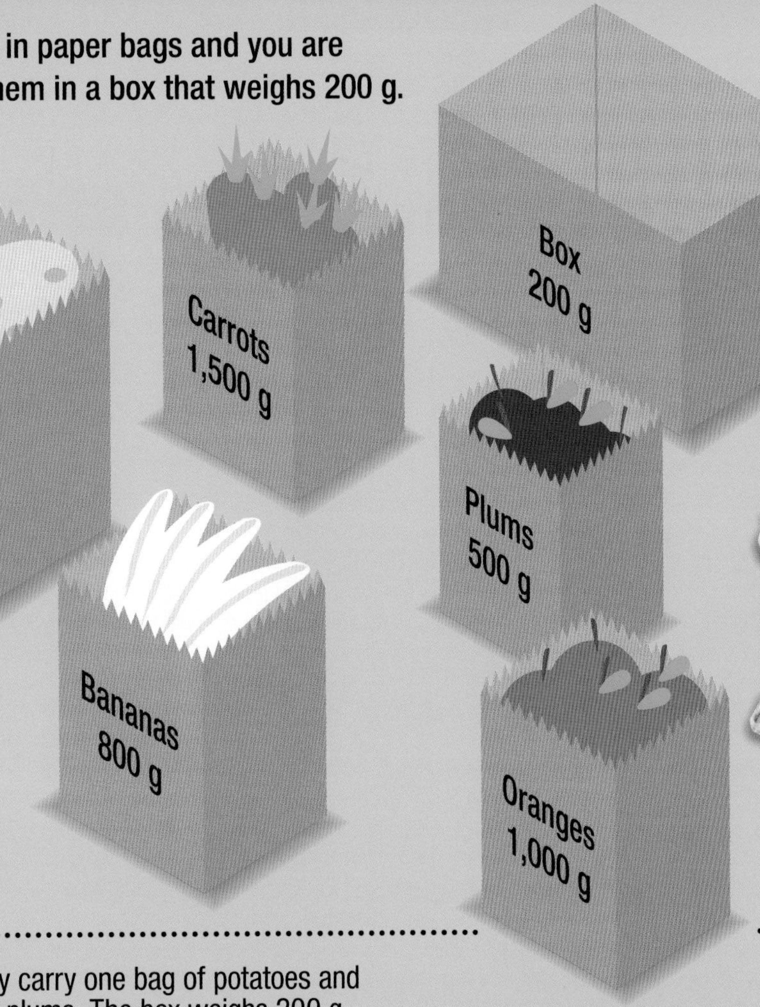

There are 1,000 g in 1 kg.

1. You can easily carry one bag of potatoes and three bags of plums. The box weighs 200 g. How much are you carrying?

2. Next, you try to lift two bags of carrots, two bags of bananas, and one bag of oranges—but it is too heavy. You tip out half a bag of oranges. How much are you carrying? (Do not forget the box!)

3. Most children in your class can carry 4 kg plus a box. There are 8 bags of carrots, 10 bags of potatoes, 15 bunches of bananas, 14 bags of plums, and 13 bags of oranges. How many children are needed to carry all this fruit and vegetables?

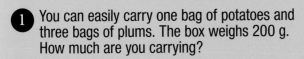

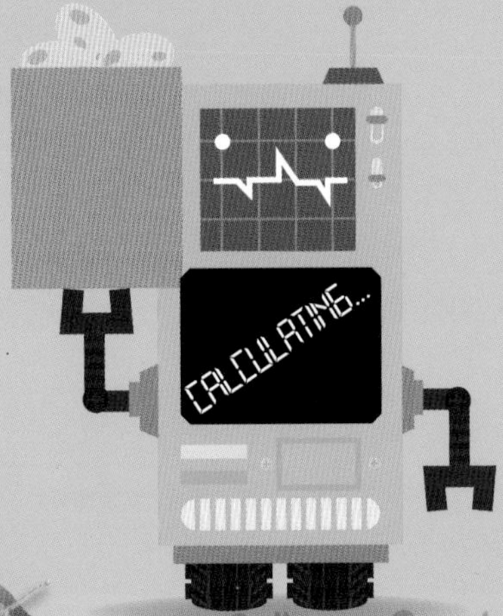

MISSION 5

MEASURE ME

You are looking at the sizes of parts of your body and working them out as **fractions** of each other.

LEARN ABOUT IT

WORKING WITH FRACTIONS

Fractions show parts of a whole. Each fraction is made up of two parts—a numerator **and a** denominator**.**

numerator → $1/2$ ← denominator

To add or subtract fractions with the same denominator, just add or subtract the numerators:

$$3/7 - 1/7 = 2/7$$

Sometimes you need to add or subtract fractions with different denominators. To do this you need to convert the fractions so that they have the same denominator, known as the **common denominator**.

$$1/3 + 1/4$$

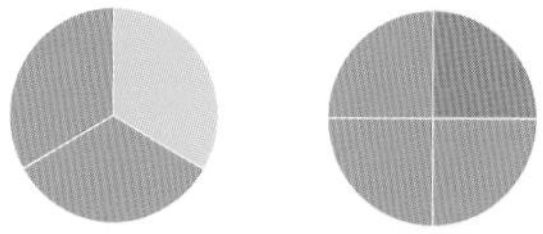

To find the common denominator, multiply the two denominators together. So for this problem:

$3 \times 4 = 12$ is the common denominator

To convert the fractions to the common denominator so that they do not change their **value**, multiply the numerators of each fraction by the denominator from the other fraction. So:

$$1/3 = \frac{1 \times 4}{12} = 4/12$$

$$1/4 = \frac{1 \times 3}{12} = 3/12$$

Then, when both numbers have the same denominator, you can simply add or subtract the numerators to get the result:

$$4/12 + 3/12 = 7/12$$

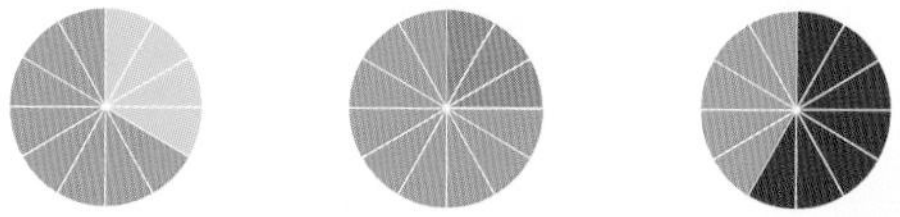

To multiply two fractions, multiply the two top numbers together and the two bottom numbers together:

$$\frac{1}{2} \times \frac{1}{4} = \frac{1 \times 1}{2 \times 4} = \frac{1}{8}$$

To divide a fraction by a whole number, multiply the denominator by the whole number. For example:

$\frac{4}{5} \div 2$ Multiply the denominator by whole number: $\frac{4}{5 \times 2} = \frac{4}{10}$

This fraction can be simplified to find the final answer:

$$\frac{4}{10} = \frac{2}{5}$$

›GO FIGURE!

Andrew has helped you measure parts of your body and has worked out some fractions.

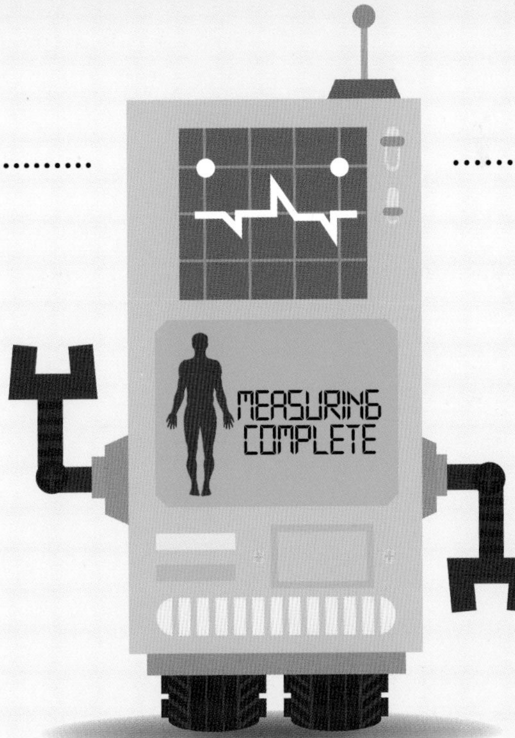

1. Your big toe is $\frac{1}{3}$ the width of your foot. What fraction of your foot do the other toes occupy all together?
2. What fraction is taken up by each smaller toe?
3. Your head is $\frac{1}{6}$ of your height. Your legs are $\frac{1}{2}$ of your height. What fraction is left for the rest of your body?
4. Your teacher's head is $\frac{1}{8}$ of her height. The distance from her knees to the ground is $\frac{1}{4}$ of her height. What fraction is the rest of her body?

MISSION 6

COMPARING BODIES

The children in your grade come in many different shapes and sizes and you want to compare the data you have collected on each student.

LEARN ABOUT IT
AVERAGES

When you have a collection of values, it is often useful to work out the average. This gives you a guide as to what is a normal value, and helps you judge whether some values are not average.

This table shows the shoe sizes of five children in your class:

Child	Shoe size
Jo	2
Chris	4
Dan	3
Julie	2
Ed	4

To calculate the average, or the **mean**, first add up the shoe sizes:

$$2 + 4 + 3 + 2 + 4 = 15$$

Then divide the total by the number of children:

$$15 \div 5 = 3$$

From this, you can see that the average shoe size of these five children is 3. A shoe size bigger than 3 is bigger than the average shoe size for this group.

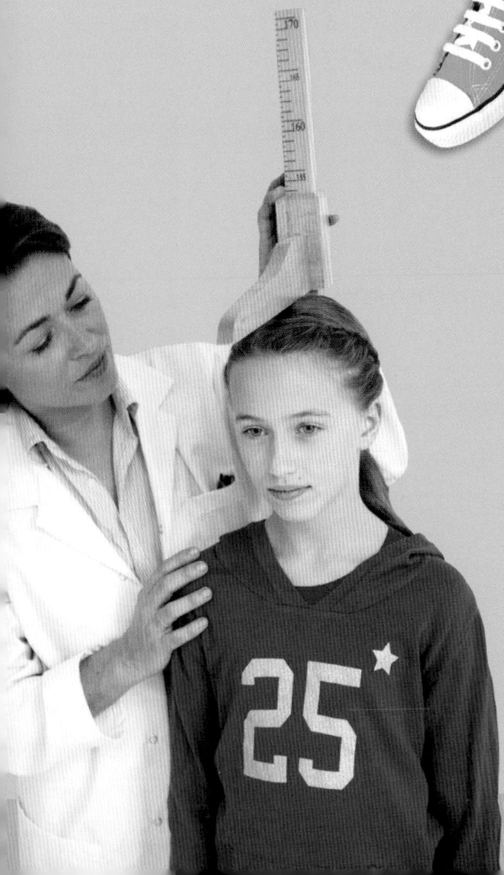

›GO FIGURE!

You have collected information about groups of children from two classes and made two tables of data. You want to find out the average weight and height of the children you have studied.

CLASS A - NAME	HEIGHT (IN.)	WEIGHT (LB)
ABIGAIL	48	68
BEN	52	79
EMILIA	50	77
HARRY	49	73
ABDUL	51	77

CLASS B - NAME	HEIGHT (IN.)	WEIGHT (LB)
CARRIE	47	64
ELISE	49	68
JIANG	46	62
TODD	48	64
SHAH	50	73

1. Work out the average height of your friends in class A.

2. Without doing the calculation, do you think the average weight of children in class A will be larger or smaller than the average weight of children in class B?

3. What is the average height of all the children, putting both classes together?

MISSION 7

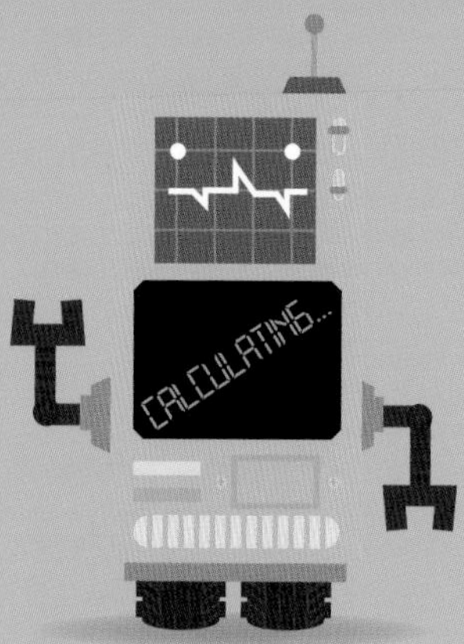

SKIN SURFACES

Andrew has measured your teacher's skin surface **area** and the skin surface area of two students in your class.

LEARN ABOUT IT
DECIMALS AND FRACTIONS

Decimal **fractions are tenths, hundredths, thousandths, and so on.**

0.1 is a tenth: $^{1}/_{10}$

0.01 is a hundredth: $^{1}/_{100}$

0.001 is a thousandth: $^{1}/_{1,000}$

The blue shaded area shows $^{4}/_{10}$ or 0.4 of the total area:

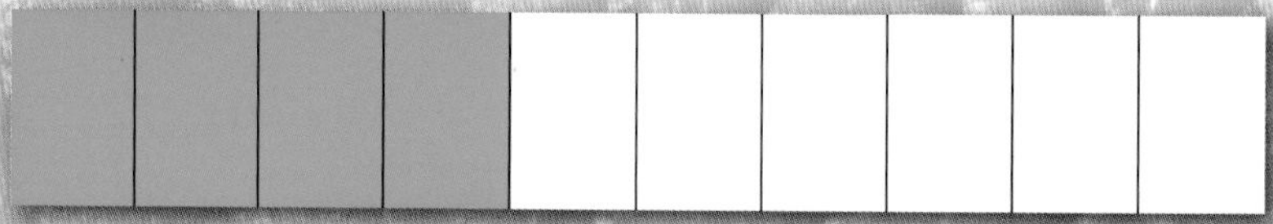

Here are some common fractions as decimals:

$^{1}/_{2}$ = 0.5
This is $^{5}/_{10}$.

$^{1}/_{5}$ = 0.2
This is $^{2}/_{10}$.

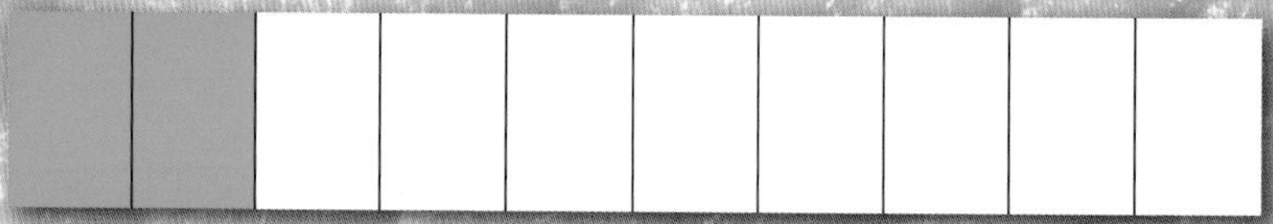

$^{1}/_{4}$ = 0.25
This is $^{25}/_{100}$.
The place value of the numbers "2" and "5" show that it is $^{2}/_{10}$ + $^{5}/_{100}$.

Some fractions cannot be written accurately as decimal fractions.

$1/3 = 0.3333...$ and the 3's keep going.

$1/6 = 0.1666...$ and the 6's keep going.

These are called **recurring** decimals.

›GO FIGURE!

This diagram shows the area of skin on your teacher. The first row shows 1 m^2. The shaded part of the second row shows a fraction of 1 m^2.

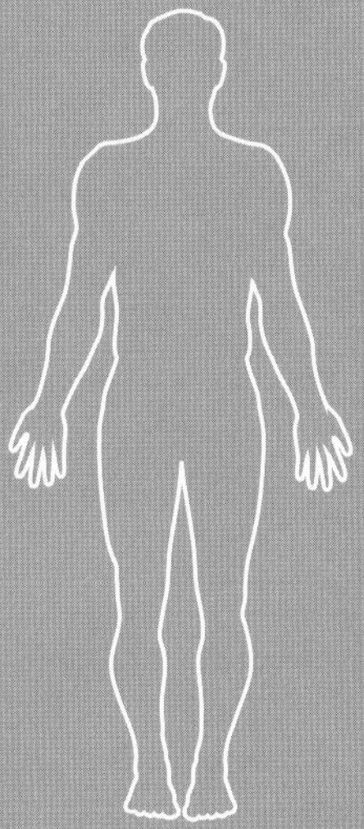

STUDENT	SKIN AREA
Holly	1.2 m^2
Ramiz	1.3 m^2

1. What is the total area of the teacher's skin, as shown by the shaded area of the two rows?

2. In your notepad, draw rows of blocks and shade the areas to show the area of Holly's skin and Ramiz's skin.

3. What are the areas of Holly's skin and Ramiz's skin written as fractions?

4. For Holly, you have shaded 1 m^2 and a fraction of a square meter. Is the fraction more than, less than, or equal to a quarter? Is it more than, less than, or equal to one-fifth?

5. What is the total area of skin on all three people together?

BARE BONES

Andrew has been counting and measuring your bones using his X-ray viewer. He has printed paper copies for you to put together a map of your skeleton, making a note of how many bones each body part has.

LEARN ABOUT IT
USING EXPRESSIONS AND EQUATIONS

An expression **uses numbers, operators (+, -, x, ÷), and** variables **to show the relationship between values. Variables are letters used to stand for a number.**

You have ten fingers (including your thumbs), each with a certain number of bones, but you have lost three bone pictures. Use the letter "a" to show the number of bones in each finger.

You could write the expression:

$$10a - 3$$

to show how many finger bone pictures you have left. It does not matter how many bones each finger has—the expression is still true.

If you want to work out how many bones there are in each finger, and you know how many bone pictures you have left, you can use this to write an equation. If you have 27 bone pictures left, the equation would be:

$$10a - 3 = 27$$

To solve the equation, you need to have the variable "a" on its own on one side of the equals sign, with the answer on the other. To do this, you need to reverse the operations (+, –, x, ÷), but you need to do this to both sides of the equation. As "3" is being subtracted in the equation, the first task is to do the reverse of this—add "3." So:

$$10a - 3 + 3 = 27 + 3$$

which is equal to

$$10a = 27 + 3$$

which is equal to

$$10a = 30$$

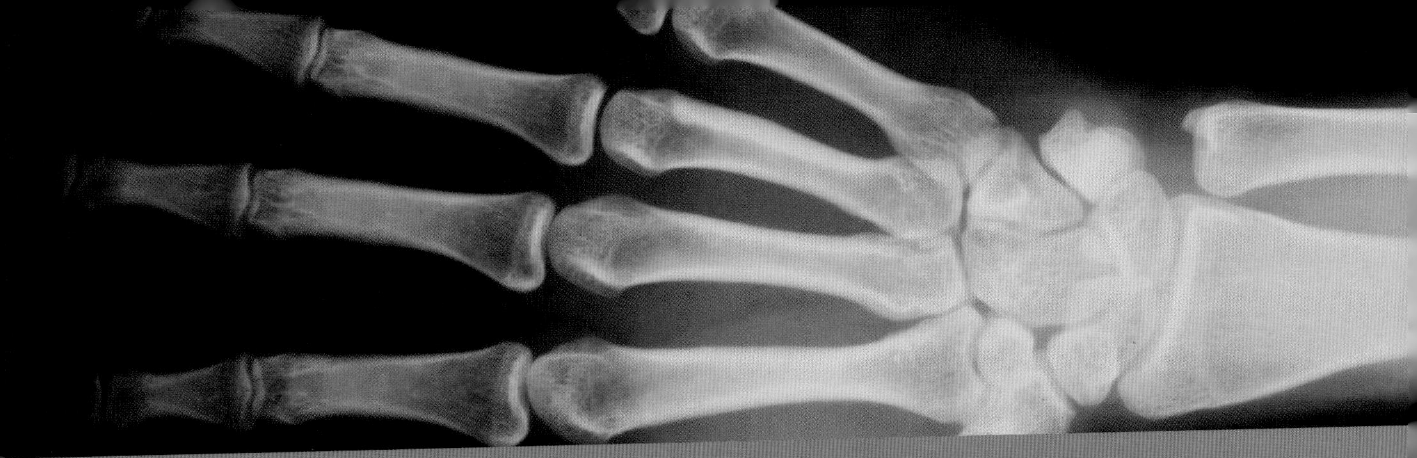

Because "a" is being multiplied by "10," the next task is to divide both sides of the equation by "10." So:

$$10a \div 10 = 30 \div 10$$

which is equal to

$$a = 3$$

So there are three bones in each finger.

›GO FIGURE!

You have laid out the printed images of your bones, but some of the pictures are missing.

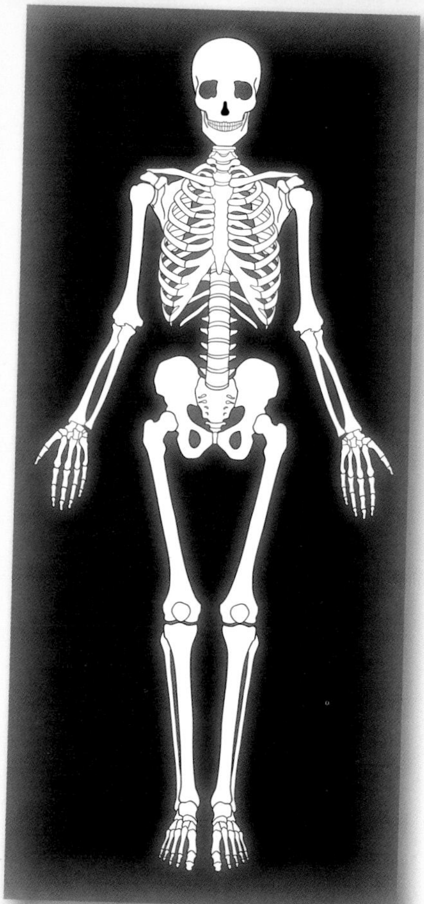

1. You can only find 13 of the 24 printed ribs. If "r" is the number of lost ribs, write an equation you could use to work out the value of "r."
2. Solve the equation you have written.
3. If "t" stands for the number of bones in one toe, write an expression showing the total number of toe bones in one foot.
4. The value of "t" is 3; how many toe bones do you have in one foot?
5. The bones in your spine are in groups. This expression shows how they are grouped:

   $7 + 12 + s + 9$

   If you have 33 bones in your spine, what is the value of "s"?

MISSION 9

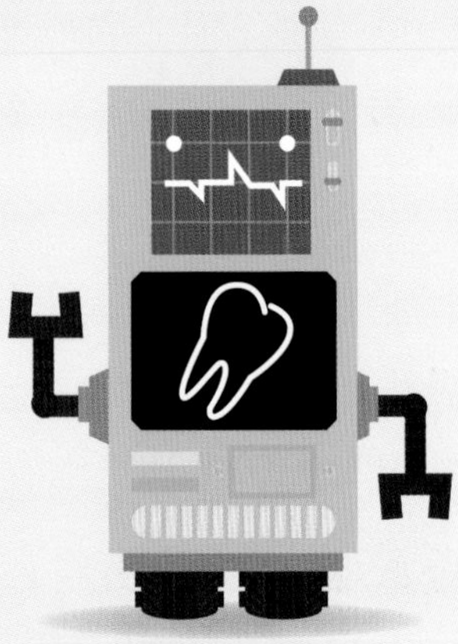

BODY RATIOS

You have counted how many baby and adult teeth your friends have, as well as any gaps, so you can study the **ratios** between the results.

LEARN ABOUT IT RATIOS

Ratios show how one quantity relates to another.

For example, if you made a drink by mixing one cup of orange juice with two cups of apple juice, the juices would be measured in the ratio:

1:2

This shows that you need twice as much apple juice as orange juice. The ratio is the same no matter how much of the drink you make.

If eight children in your class have blonde hair and six children have brown hair, you can say that the ratio of blonde hair to brown is 8:6.

As with fractions, you can simplify ratios—so 8:6 is the same as 4:3. These ratios are equivalent.

$$8:6 = 4:3$$

In a different class with the same ratio of blonde- to brown-haired children, you could use the ratio 4:3 to work out quantities. So if there were 12 children with blonde hair in the other class, you can work out the number of children with brown hair.

To do this, you divide the total by the ratio value that relates to children with blonde hair:

$$12 \div 4 = 3$$

You then multiply this number by the ratio value that relates to children with brown hair to get the answer:

$$3 \times 3 = 9$$

So there are 9 children with brown hair in the other class.

›GO FIGURE!

Andrew has made some computer models of students' mouths. All baby teeth are white and all adult teeth are yellow. Gaps are shown in blue. Here is Andrew's model for your friend Lily.

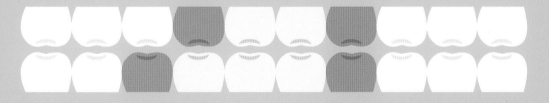

1. What is the ratio of baby teeth to adult teeth in Lily's mouth?
2. On average, the children in your class each have 25 teeth, 10 of which are adult teeth. What is the ratio of adult teeth to baby teeth?
3. Travis has 16 adult teeth. If you used the adult to baby teeth ratio of 4:3, how many baby teeth does he have?
4. Angus has $^{3}/_{24}$ gaps, and $^{6}/_{24}$ adult teeth. Change the fractions to their lowest terms. What is the ratio of gaps to adult teeth?

MISSION 10

BIGGER AND BIGGER

You have been measuring the height of your friend Toby every month for six months to study trends and the rate at which he is growing.

LEARN ABOUT IT
TABLES, TRENDS, AND GRAPHS

Sometimes, data follows a clear trend, making a pattern.

This sequence shows the numbers increasing by 2 each time:

1, 3, 5, 7, 9, 11

Add 2 to get the next number.

This sequence shows the numbers doubling each time:

1, 2, 4, 8, 16, 32

The number doubles with each step.

This graph and table show how a person's temperature varies over 10 hours:

A sequence of continuous data is best shown as a **line graph**. You can plot each item of data from the set or table on the graph and draw a line joining the points. You can read off values between the data points to work out values that were not measured.

Hour	°C
4:00 am	37.0
6:00 am	37.1
8:00 am	37.2
10:00 am	37.2
12 noon	37.3
2:00 pm	37.4

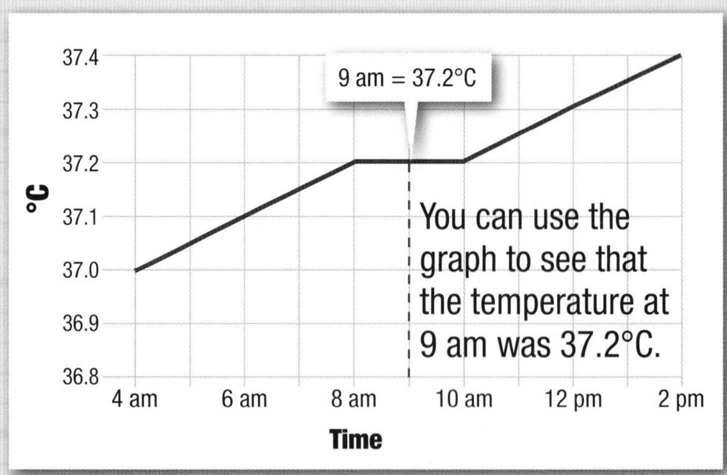

›GO FIGURE!

It is the end of your study and you are looking at your figures. But you cannot find your record of Toby's height in April and May.

MONTH	HEIGHT (CM)
February	105 cm
March	105.6 cm
April	
May	
June	107.4 cm
July	108 cm
August	108.6 cm

1. Which type of graph would be best to show Toby's growth?
   - Pie graph
   - Bar graph
   - Line graph
2. If Toby grew steadily, what would his height be in April and May?
3. In your notepad, draw a graph of Toby's growth.
4. Another friend has measured Toby's sister Hannah's growth and drawn a graph (see below). Draw a table like the one above by reading data from the graph.

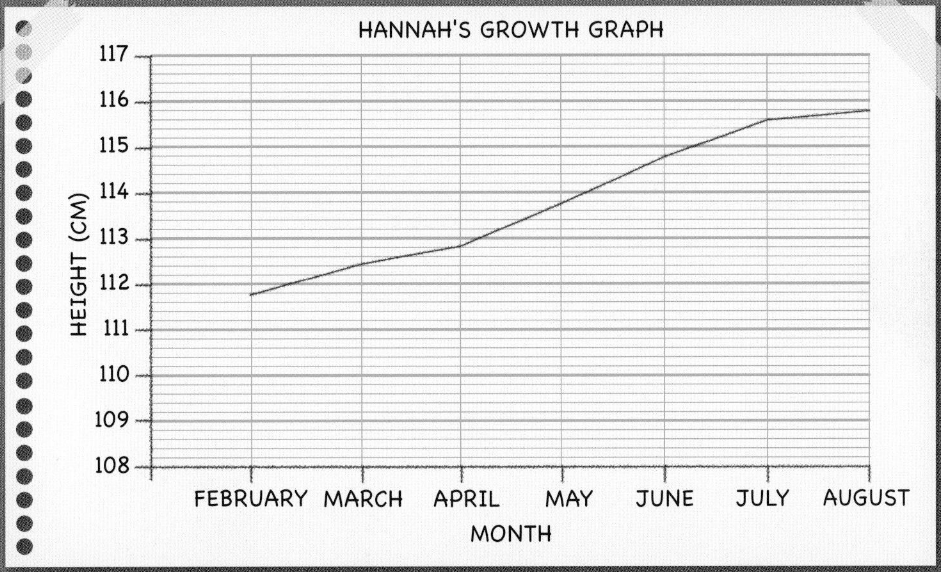

MISSION 11

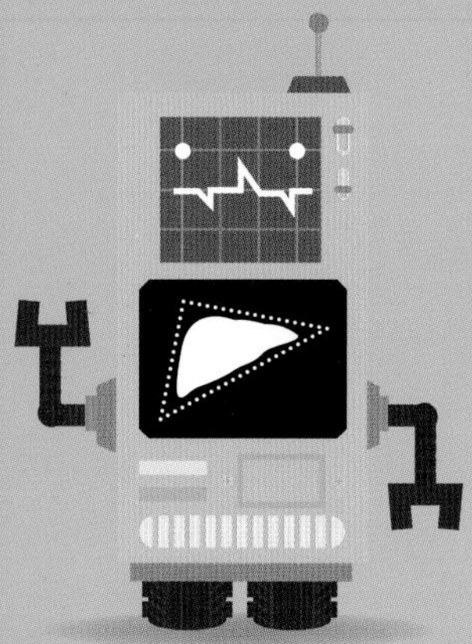

TRIANGLES INSIDE YOU!

Sometimes it helps to find the areas of objects by replacing them with simple shapes to make the calculations easier. The simplest shape of all is the **triangle**.

LEARN ABOUT IT TRIANGLES

Two triangles are congruent **if they have the same angles and all the sides are the same size.**

Congruent triangles can be rotated, flipped, or moved. If you cut out two congruent triangles from paper, you could lay one exactly over the other with no overlap.

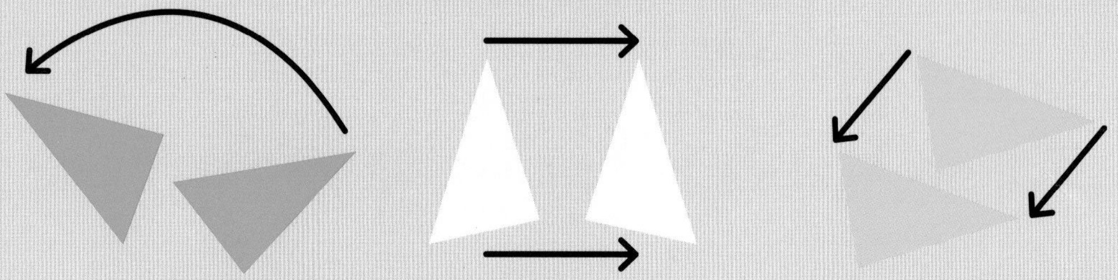

Rotated   Flipped (reflected)   Moved (translated)

Triangles are similar if they have the same angles, but they are different sizes. The sides will be in proportion—that is, the ratio between the sides will be the same.

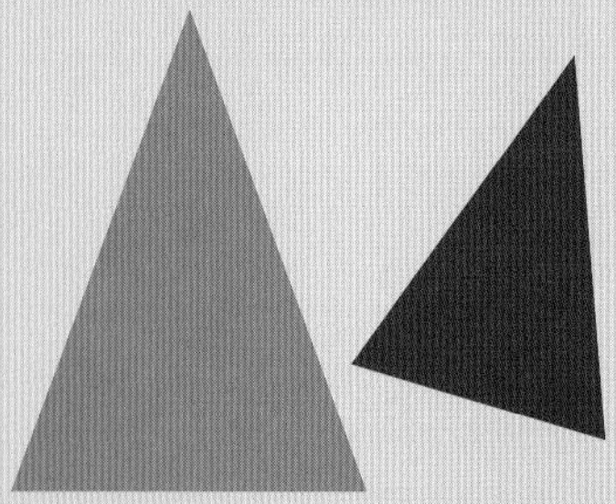

Similar triangles are still similar if one has been rotated, flipped, or moved.

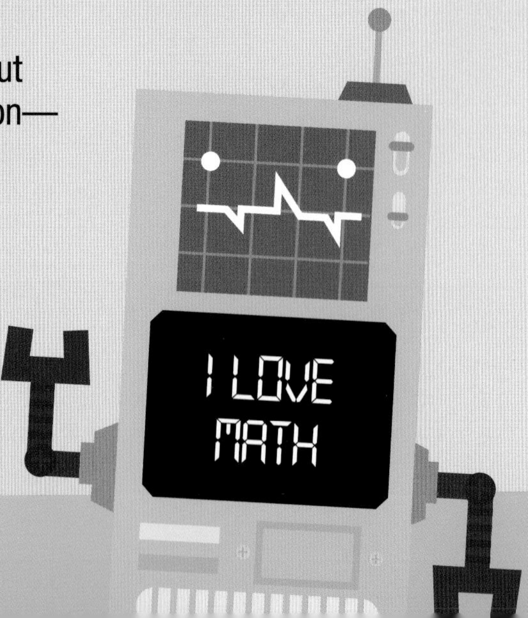

Use this formula to work out the area of a triangle:

½ x base x height

½ x 10 x 5 = ½ x 50 = 25 cm²

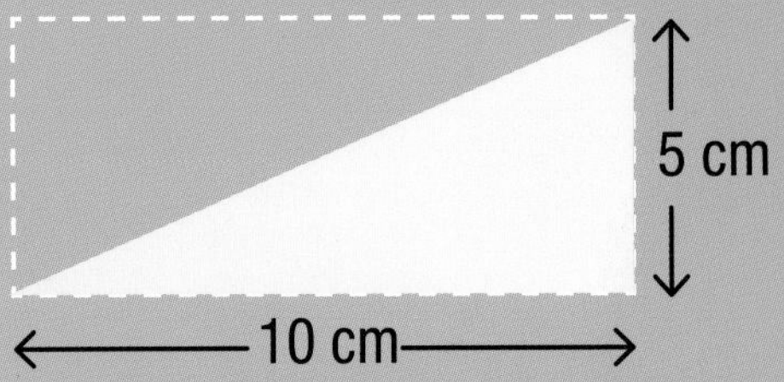

The **perimeter** of any triangle is the sum of all the sides:

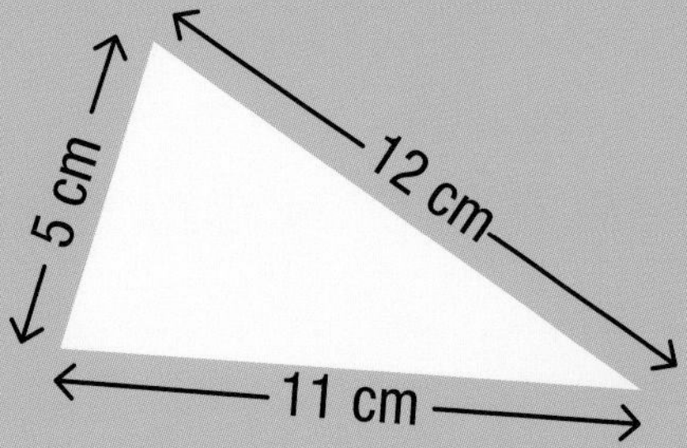

Perimeter =
5 + 11 + 12 = 28 cm

›GO FIGURE!

Andrew has taken measurements of your liver and the livers of four of your friends. To help you compare the size and shape, he has drawn triangles around them.

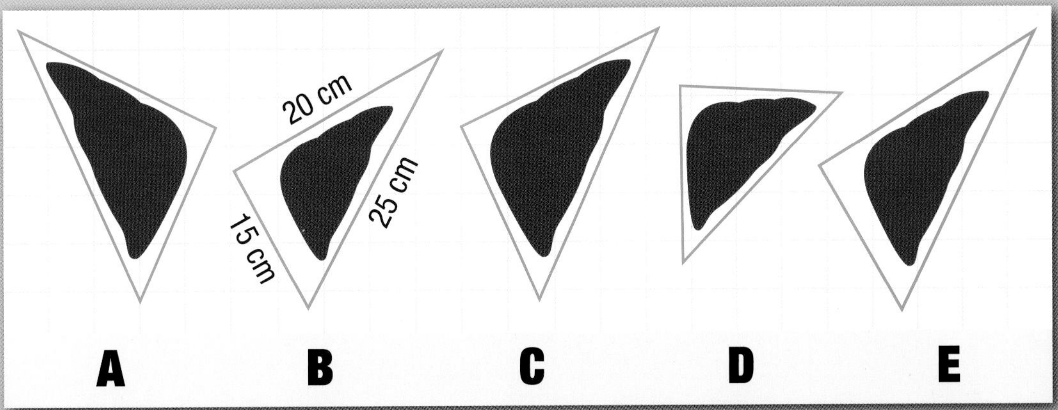

1. What is the approximate area of the triangle around liver B?
2. What is the perimeter of the triangle around liver B?
3. Which two livers are shown inside congruent triangles? Use your ruler to check the lengths of the sides.
4. Which two livers are shown inside similar triangles?

MISSION 11

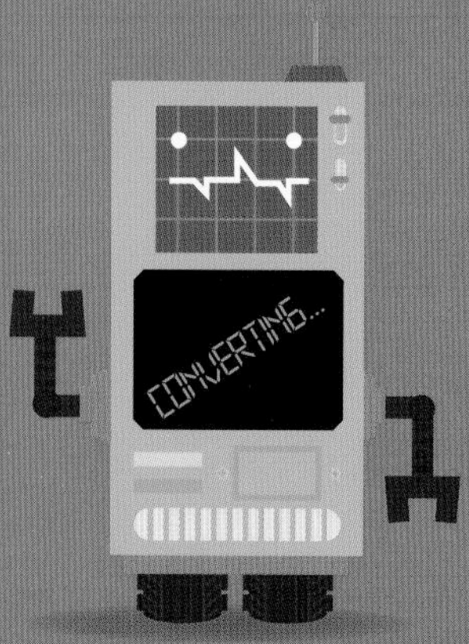

SHARING DATA

You have been explaining your human body project to your grandmother and want to share some of your data with her.

LEARN ABOUT IT
CONVERT IMPERIAL AND METRIC UNITS

Metric **units work in multiples of 10 and are easy to use in calculations.**

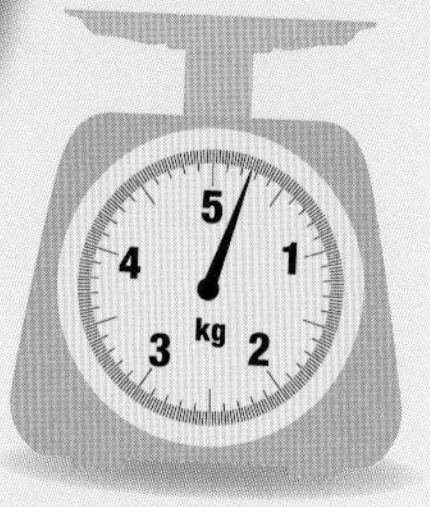

1 kilogram	=	1,000 grams (g)
1 kilometer	=	1,000 meters (m)
1 meter	=	100 centimeters (cm)
1 centimeter	=	10 millimeters (mm)

Imperial units are not multiples of 10. As a result, they are more complicated to use in calculations.

1 pound	=	16 ounces (oz)
1 mile	=	1,760 yards (yd)
1 yard	=	3 feet (ft)
1 foot	=	12 inches (in)

All scientific work uses metric units, but some people use imperial units. To convert between imperial and metric units, you can use these approximate values:

IMPERIAL		METRIC
1 inch	=	2.5 centimeters
1 yard	=	0.9 meters
1 mile	=	1.6 kilometers
2.2 pounds	=	1 kilogram

If a boy weighing 40 kg went for a 2 km run, you could convert this to imperial units:

40 kg = 40 x 2.2 = 88 lbs
2 km ÷ 1.6 = 1.25 miles

To convert the other way, you reverse the operation, so you divide instead of multiply, and multiply instead of divide:

88 lbs ÷ 2.2 = 40 kg
1.25 mi x 1.6 = 2 km

›GO FIGURE!

Andrew has compiled the data for you. He has used metric units for all the measurements. However, your relative uses imperial units and wants the data converted to these.

	MEASUREMENT	ROUNDED	METRIC MEASURE	IMPERIAL MEASURE
Height	1,354 mm	_____(nearest 10)	_____cm	_____inches
Weight	30,387 g	___(nearest 1,000)	_____kg	_____lbs
Waist size	612 mm	_____(nearest 10)	_____cm	_____inches
Longest run	269,890 mm	_(nearest 10,000)	_____m	_____yards

1. In your notepad, copy the table and fill in the second column, rounding the measurements as instructed.
2. Convert each rounded figure to the metric unit in the third column.
3. Convert each metric figure in column three to the imperial unit in column four using the conversion figures on page 26.

ANSWERS

04-05 Your whole body

1. 5, 2, 467

2. 1, 2, 13, 26

3. 467 + 285,324 = 285,791
Odd; whenever you add an odd and an even number, the answer is odd.

4. 8. Its value is 80,000.

5.

Hundred Thousands	Ten Thousands	Thousands	Hundreds	Tens	Ones
2	8	5	3	2	4

200,000+
80,000+
5,000+
300+
20+
4

06-07 Eating well

1. Tuesday and Thursday

2. Monday, Wednesday, Saturday

3.

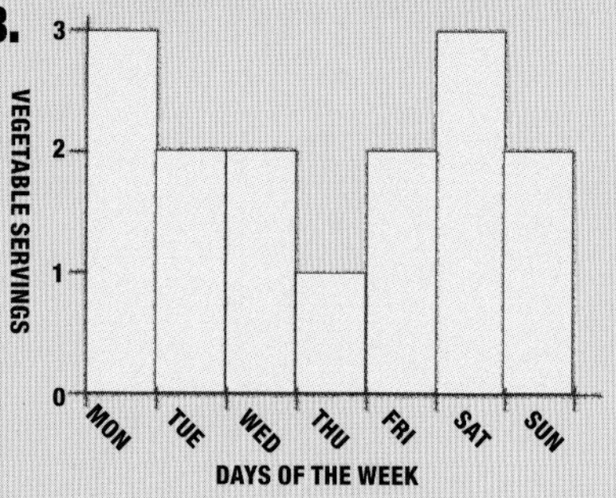

4. Monday and Saturday

5. Table A

08-09 Breathe in, breathe out

1. 100% - (78% + 1%) =
100% - 79% = 21%

2. 100% - (78% + 16% + 1%) =
100% - 95% = 5%

3.

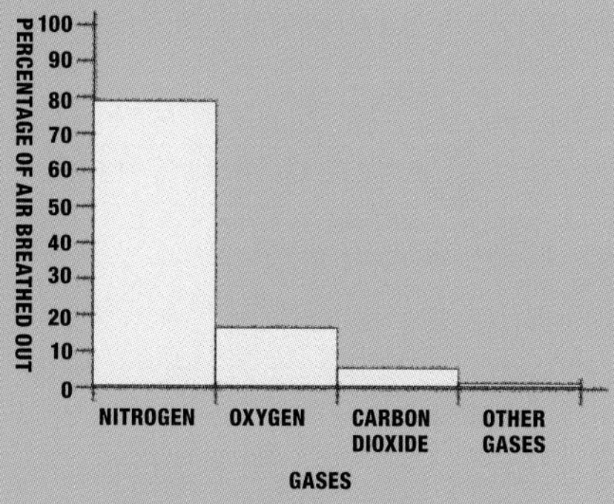

4. (21 ÷ 100) x 600 = 126 cm^3

10-11 Heavy lifting

1. (1 x 2,000) + (3 x 500) + 200 g =
2,000 + 1,500 + 200 = 3,700 g (3.7 kg)

2. (2 x 1,500) + (2 x 800) + (1 x 1,000) – (0.5 x 1,000) = 3,000 + 1,600 + 1,000 – 500 = 5,100 g (5.1 kg) + 200g = 5,300 g (5.3 kg)

3. The total weight is:
(8 x 1,500) + (10 x 2,000) + (15 x 800) + (14 x 500) + (13 x 1,000) =
12,000 + 20,000 + 12,000 + 7,000 + 13,000 = 64,000 g = 64 kg
64 ÷ 4 = 16
So you need 16 children

12-13 Body measurements

1. $1 - \frac{1}{3} = \frac{3}{3} - \frac{1}{3} = \frac{2}{3}$

2. $\frac{2}{3} \div 4 = \frac{2}{12} = \frac{1}{6}$

3. $\frac{1}{6} + \frac{1}{2} = \frac{2}{12} + \frac{6}{12} = \frac{8}{12} = \frac{2}{3}$;
$1 - \frac{2}{3} = \frac{3}{3} - \frac{2}{3} = \frac{1}{3}$ is left for the rest of your body

4. $\frac{1}{8} + \frac{1}{4} = \frac{4}{32} + \frac{8}{32} = \frac{12}{32} = \frac{3}{8}$; $1 - \frac{3}{8} = \frac{5}{8}$ is left for the rest of her body

14-15 Comparing bodies

1. 48 + 52 + 50 + 49 + 51 = 250
250 ÷ 5 = 50 inches

2. Larger – most of the children in class A are heavier. Most of the children in class A weigh more than 70 lbs, while most in class B weigh less than 70 lbs.

3. 250 in. (total height of class A) + 240 in. (total height of class B) = 490 in.
490 ÷ 10 (total number of children) = 49 inches

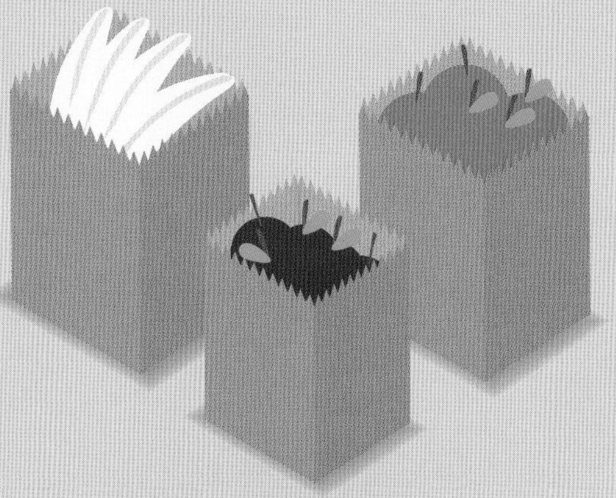

16-17 Skin surfaces

1. 1.8 m^2
2.

Holly

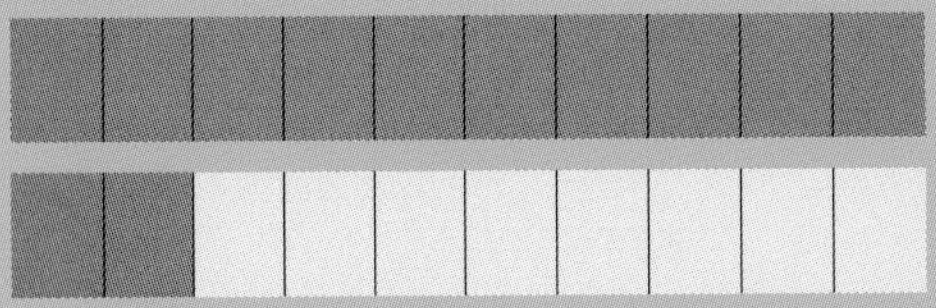

Ramiz

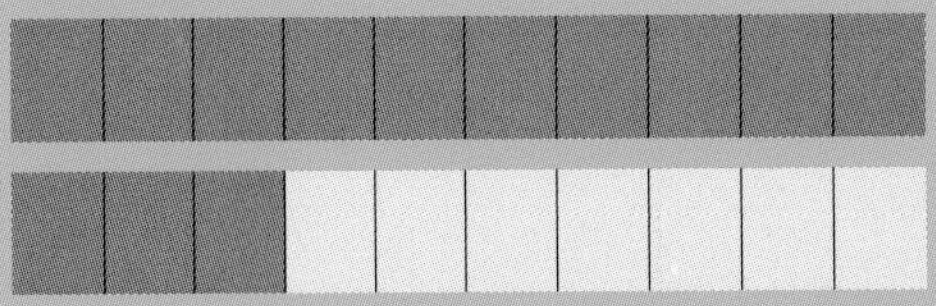

3. Holly: $1^2/_{10}$ or $1^1/_5$ m^2; Ramiz $1^3/_{10}$ m^2
4. Less than a quarter; equal to a fifth
5. 1.8 + 1.2 + 1.3 = 4.3 m^2

18-19 Bare bones

1. 24 – 13 = r or 24 – r = 13 or r + 13 = 24
2. 24 – 13 = 11 = r
3. 5t
4. 5 x 3 = 15
5. 7 + 12 + s + 9 – 7 – 12 – 9 = 33 – 7 – 12 – 9, so s = 5

20-21 Body ratios

1. 11:5
2. 25 – 10 = 15, so 10:15 which equals 2:3
3. 16 ÷ 4 = 4; 4 x 3 = 12 baby teeth
4. $^3/_{24}$ = $^1/_8$ gaps; $^6/_{24}$ = $^1/_4$ adult teeth. The ratio is 3:6, which is 1:2

22-23 Bigger and bigger

1. Line graph – because it shows continuous data best.
2. Toby's height increases by 0.6 cm per month, so the missing figures are April—106.2 cm and May—106.8 cm.
3.

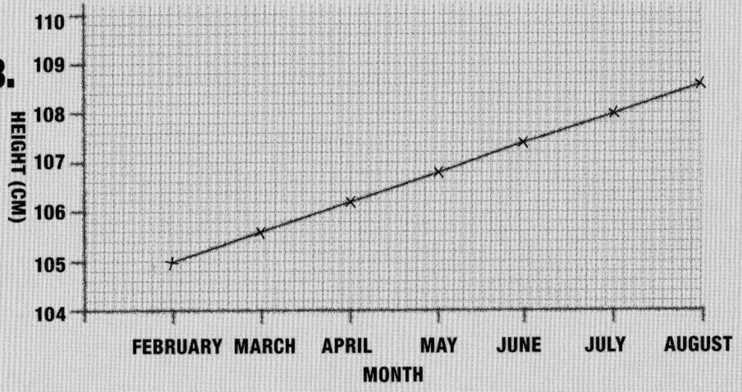

4.

MONTH	HEIGHT (CM)
February	111.8
March	112.2
April	112.8
May	113.8
June	114.8
July	115.6
August	115.8

24-25 Triangles inside you!

1. ½ x 20 x 15 = ½ x 300 = 150 cm^2
2. 15 + 20 + 25 = 60 cm
3. A and C; they have the same angles and sides
4. B and E; they have the same angles, but are different sizes

26-27 Sharing data

1.

	MEASUREMENT	ROUNDED	METRIC MEASURE	IMPERIAL MEASURE
Height	1,354 mm	1,350 mm	135 cm	54 inches
Weight	30,387 g	30,000 g	30 kg	66 lbs
Waist size	612 mm	610 mm	61 cm	24.4 inches
Longest run	269,890 mm	270,000 mm	270 m	300 yards

MATH GLOSSARY

ADD
Combine two numbers to produce a third. If two positive numbers are added, then the resulting number will be bigger.

AREA
The amount of two-dimensional space covered by a shape or object

AXIS
A line that is used in math to locate a point

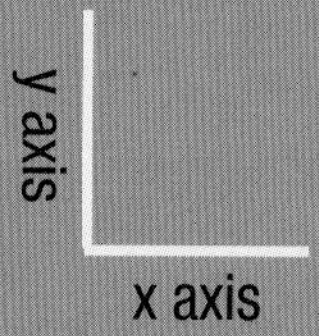

BAR GRAPH
A chart that uses bars to show values from a set of data. The height of each bar reflects the value of one item of data.

COMMON DENOMINATOR
When the denominators in two or more fractions are the same

CONGRUENT
When objects have exactly the same shape and size

DATA
A collection of facts or information

DECIMAL
Dividing whole numbers into smaller units. One can be divided into ten decimals (tenths), and these can be divided into ten smaller decimals (hundredths), and so on.

DENOMINATOR
The bottom number in a fraction

EQUATION
An expression that can be solved. An equation has two sides to it, which are linked with an equals symbol, or another symbol to show an inequality between the two sides.

EVEN NUMBER
A number that can be divided by 2

EXPRESSION
A way of showing the relationship between two amounts

FACTOR
A factor of a number is a whole number that can be divided exactly into it. For example, 3 is a factor of 6, because $6 \div 3 = 2$.

FRACTION
A part of a whole number. Fractions use one number on top of another.

IMPERIAL
A system of measuring units which uses various multiples for different units. For example, there are 12 inches in 1 foot.

LINE GRAPH
A type of graph which shows a sequence of data, connecting the values with a continuous line

MEAN
A calculated average of a group of numbers. Add the numbers together and divide by how many numbers there are to find the mean.

METRIC
A scientific system of measurement in which units are all related to each other by multiples of 10. For example, there are 10 mm in 1 cm, and 100 cm in 1 m.

NUMERATOR
The top number in a fraction

ODD NUMBER
A number that cannot be divided by 2

PERCENTAGE
A percentage shows one number as a fraction of another number, given in hundredths. Each percentage point represents $^{1}/_{100\,th}$ of the total.

PERIMETER
The total distance around a shape

PLACE VALUE
The position of a digit within a number which defines its value. For example, a three-digit number has, from right to left, ones, tens, and hundreds.

PRIME NUMBER
A number that can be divided only by itself and 1

RATIO
Ratios show how one number or value is related to another. So a ratio of 2:1 shows that there are twice as many of the first value as there are of the second.

RECURRING
When something repeats itself forever

SUBTRACTING
Take one number away from another to produce a third. If a positive number is subtracted from another positive number, then the resulting number will be smaller.

TABLE
A way of laying out numbers and information in rows and columns

TRIANGLE
A shape with three sides. There are three types of triangle. An equilateral triangle has all three sides and angles the same. An isosceles has two of its sides and angles the same. A scalene triangle has all three sides and angles that are all different.

VALUE
An amount represented by a number

VARIABLE
Something that can have a range of possible values. Variables are usually shown in expressions or equations using a letter.

LEARNING MORE

WEBSITES

www.mathisfun.com
A huge website packed full of explanations, examples, games, puzzles, activities, worksheets, and teacher resources for all age levels.

http://ca.ixl.com/math/grade-4
Practice your math skills by answering questions in various categories. The questions will automatically get harder as you improve!

www.mathplayground.com
An action-packed website with math games, mathematical word problems, worksheets, puzzles, and videos.

INDEX

adding 4, 10
averages 14, 15

bar graphs 6, 7

common denominators 12

decimals 16, 17
denominators 12, 13

equations 18, 19
even numbers 4, 5
expressions 18, 19

factors 4, 5
fractions 12, 13, 16, 17

graphs 22, 23

imperial units 26, 27

line graphs 22, 23

metric units 26, 27
mixed operations 10, 11
multiplying 10

numerators 12

odd numbers 4, 5

percentages 8, 9
prime numbers 4, 5

ratios 20, 21
recurring decimals 17

sequences 22, 23
subtracting 10

tables 6, 7, 15, 22, 23
trends 22, 23
triangles 24, 25

variables 18, 19